YOGINI IN MY MUSIC

UNLOCKING THE MYSTERIES OF MUSIC & SPIRITUALITY

Nadhamuni Gayatri Bharat

Copyright © 2023 by Nadhamuni Gayatri Bharat

All rights reserved. No part of this publication may be reproduced, distributed, or transmitted in any form or by any means, including photocopying, recording, or other electronic or mechanical methods, without the prior written permission of the publisher, except in the case of brief quotations embodied in critical reviews and certain other noncommercial uses permitted by copyright law.

Book Design by Aeyshaa
Cover Design - Rose Miller
Covert Art "Yogini' - "Theganeshastore.etsy.com"
Copy Editing & Proofreading - Tiffany S (UK)

Contents

- INVOCATION 4
- H.H. PUJYASRI. NADHAMUNI NARAYANA AYYANGAR 6
- DEDICATION 8
- ACKNOWLEDGMENT 9
- EPIGRAPH 10
- ABOUT THE AUTHOR 11
- PREFACE 13

1. THE BEGINNING 18
   - THE CONCERT 19
   - SIDDHA PURUSHA 22

2. TRANSCENDENT 26
   - THE FIRST "ANUBHOOTHI" 27

3. LIFE UNFOLDS 33
   - KALI – GODDESS OF TIME & CHANGE 34
   - FIRE 38

4. INTENSE THAPAS 43
   - CONSCIOUSNESS 44
   - BHAVA AAVESHAM 48
   - SEVA THROUGH MUSIC 53

5. SURRENDER 57
   - ERADICATING THE KARMAS 58
   - DREAMS 60

6. CONCLUSION 63
   - MITHRA 64

- REQUEST TO THE READER 71

INVOCATION

*sac-cid-ānanda-rūpāya viśvotpaty-ādi-hetave | *tāpa-traya-vināśāya śrī-kṛṣṇāya vayaṁ Numaha ||* - PADMA PURANAM

We offer our Humble obeisances unto Lord Sri Krishna, whose transcendental form is Truth, Knowledge, and Bliss personified. He is the cause of the creation, maintenance and destruction of the universe and the destroyer of the three types of miseries.

Sarva-Mangala-Maangalye Shive Sarvaartha-Saadhike | Sharannye Trya[i-A]mbake Gauri Naaraayani NamostuTe || - DEVI MAHATMYAM

Salutations to You O Narayani Who is the Auspiciousness in All the Auspicious, Auspiciousness Herself, Complete with All the Auspicious Attributes, and Who fulfills All the Objectives of the Devotees (Purusharthas - Dharma, Artha, Kama, and Moksha),Who is the Giver of Refuge, With Three Eyes and a Shining Face; Salutations to You O Narayani.

* pU mannu mAdhu porundhiya mArban * pugazh malindha pA mannu mARan * adi paNindhuyndhavan * * palkalaiyOr thAm manna vandha irAmAnusan * charaNAravindham nAm manni vAzha * nenchE! solluvOm avan nAmangkaLE ||* - RAMANUJA NOOTRANDADHI

Oh our mind!! Let us recite the great name of Swami Ramanuja which is the easiest and greatest and the one which can give both Drishta and Adhrishta Phalam. Scholars who had learnt all four Vedaas and shaastra failed to realize the supreme power and took refuge at the feet of Swami Ramanuja. One who gave his entire life to the lotus feet of Swami Nammazhwar, who rendered mouthfuls of praise for the lord who bears the lotus dame Lakshmi on his chest and also followed his footsteps in experiencing the divine "Anubhavam". Let us take refuge at the lotus feet of this Swami Ramanuja who was praised by all the great scholars of shaastra.

PARAMAHAMSA NADHAMUNI NARAYANA AYYANGAR SWAMIGAL

BHOOMA NARAYANA AYYANGAR

Author's Mama & Athai

H.H. Pujyasri. Nadhamuni Narayana Ayyangar

PARAMAHAMSA NADHAMUNI Narayana Ayyangar Swamigal in his Bhajan Room

Author with her Mama

"H.H. Nadhamuni Narayana Ayyangar (Nana ji) was a mysterious mystic. Once, when I asked him about His Guru, He didn't directly answer me. I was present in his Pooja room, a close disciple of his visited him at that time. Nana ji told him to have his dinner with Him. When the visiting friend said he is in Upavasa on Fridays, for Lord Narasimha, Mama told him, "Don't worry, I will tell your Narasimha. He won't mistake you. Have your dinner, stay with me tonight and you can leave tomorrow morning. Regarding His Guru, like Dattatreya, He had several Gurus. First and foremost, I can think of Shri J Swamigal, whose instructions he would meticulously follow. There are several instances. Similarly Swami Ritajananda of Sri Ramakrishna Mutt. Swamiji has guided Him for several mystical tasks. There are many. In the course of our lengthy conversations, He had narrated many incidents concerning men and matters. He would underline the morale from each person's life. How can you explain a Vaishnava having a statue of Lord Siva in his Bhajan Hall? To me He is God in disguise"

- H. Ramakrishnan, disciple, popular newscaster, carnatic musician, konnakol artist & a journalist.

https://www.hramakrishnan.com/myguru.htm

DEDICATION

To my husband, who has walked every step of this journey with me.

To my Athai & my parents.

To my gurus, who planted the seed of knowledge in me and nurtured it.

To my daughter, who continues to inspire me to tell stories that matter.

To you, dear reader, for making this journey worthwhile.

To the past that shaped me, the present that nurtures me and the future that awaits me.

Acknowledgment

I wish to express my gratitude to Pujyashri Swamini Radhikananda Saraswati Mataji, a devoted disciple of Swami Chinmayanandaji. She served with unwavering dedication at Chinmaya Mission for 14 years, and has since wholeheartedly committed her life to spiritual pursuit and service to God.

Mataji's invaluable assistance has been instrumental in the realization of this publication.

EPIGRAPH

> "Infinite is the garment that She wears!
> She illumines the lotus of the heart"
> "Women are, all of them, the veritable images of PARASHAKTI"
> **- Swami Ramakrishna Paramahamsa**

ABOUT THE AUTHOR

Nadhamuni Gayatri Bharat, the author of this memoir, reveals her musical journey, unveiling a profound connection with the divine through her music, a secret she shares for the first time.

Readers will be spellbound by her mystical experiences, from her early life under the guidance of the Seer to her advanced training by musical stalwarts, and her ultimate reawakening to her spiritual calling.

The memoir also introduces readers to a multitude of profound spiritual insights, making it a must-read for those seeking a deeper understanding of Indian classical music and Hinduism[1], Hindu philosophies, spirituality, and mysticism.

---

1   INDIAN CLASSICAL MUSIC & HINDUISM - Music in Hinduism serves as a spiritual discipline, elevating one's inner being to divine peacefulness and bliss, reflecting the belief that the highest aim of music is to connect with the divine. Hinduism's concept of Dharma, crucial to its religious framework, upholds the universe and society, emphasizing ethical and moral duties that guide spiritual practices within the religion. Music plays a significant role in various cultures for spiritual purposes, both within and outside religious contexts, showcasing its universal application in connecting with the spiritual realm. The intersection of spirituality and music is a timeless practice in both Eastern and Western cultures, with Indian music, in particular, holding deep roots in spiritual experiences. Indian classical music, rooted in ancient traditions, showcases a rich melodic and rhythmic tapestry. Ragas and talas are fundamental elements, creating a structured and intricate framework in Indian classical music. The improvisational nature of performances allows for artistic expression and innovation within the established classical framework. The two main genres, Hindustani and Carnatic, contribute distinct regional flavors to Indian classical music. Guru-shishya parampara, the teacher-student tradition, plays a pivotal role in passing down the artistry and knowledge of Indian classical music.

"Yogini in my Music" opens a window to the mystical moments and spiritual journeys of women who balance their roles as artists and spiritual seekers within the context of Hinduism.

- https://www.facebook.com/nadhamunigayatribharat
- https://open.spotify.com/artist/3G4AWAmKvRiaJ8p3fe92tV
- https://gayatribharat.wixsite.com/website
- https://twitter.com/NadhamuniGB
- https://www.youtube.com/channel/UCY51KCno1hABuPelJ-U2umUw/featured

PREFACE

Sadhana[2] is not a journey of roses and lilies nor is it a soft and sweet process. Like how we peel away layers of an onion, sadhana is a process of ripping off all our layers, cutting off all our attachments, jealousies, desires, greed, fear, hatred, and much more. And in this arduous process the individual's physical and subtle body goes through immense pain. Only if he or she goes through this pain can they experience an elevated state of Consciousness. It is a journey one must go through to experience that state.

The term "SAdhanA" signifies accomplishment, and the term "SAdhak" can be translated as, those who earnestly practice towards achieving specific goals. While all of us could be considered as such, this memoir specifically caters to those "SAdhak" who are dedicated to spiritual practices aimed at exploring the depths of Atma and yearning for "MOKSHA[3]".

As per "ANUBANDHA CATUSTAYA[4]" those who have this "ADHIKARA[5]" can only benefit from this memoir, as the "VISHAYA"[6] is only Spirituality and Music.

A memoir written in the Tamil language can only be understood by a person who can read, speak, and understand this

---

2   SADHANA – Sadhana is an immense effort that one puts in to achieve perfection in the spiritual journey. The term Sadhana refers only to spirituality and not anything relating to these worldly things.
3   MOKSHA – Ultimate Liberation.
4   ANUBANDHA CHATUSHTAYA – The four things, after knowing which, one gets inspired to study a shastra
5   ADHIKARA - Rights
6   VISHAYA – Topic.

language. In the same way, you will be able to understand this memoir only If you are interested in spirituality, or have started on your spiritual journey; are immersed in spiritual experiences or you are a musician interested in spirituality,

The spiritual and emotional bond that I shared with my very first guru[7], my mama[8], a great Siddha Purusha[9] H.H. Nadhamuni Narayana Ayyangar[10], was profoundly special.

This memoir is a slice of my personal life events that connected me with my mama, my mystical musical moments, my intimate moments with my "ishta-deivam"[11] my state of transcendence, challenging life situations that helped me get closer to the divine, emotional, and spiritual truths.

In this material world, neither the husband nor the wife would want to share their intimate moments with a stranger, and neither would I. I never intended to share my state of transcendence or my intimate moments with my 'ishta-deivam' with anyone. After reading this memoir, I hope you will understand why I chose to write it.

I would like to first clarify 3 POINTS.

First, you can be a follower of any religion, you are most welcome to read this memoir, but you should note that if you chant the Gayatri mantra[12] one crore times, you will only get the darshan of Goddess Gayatri, not someone else because that is the sole purpose of this mantra. A mantra is not secular, mantras

---

7 GURU – He is NOT JUST A TEACHER or an EXPERT. He is beyond all these.
8 MAMA – Uncle.
9 SIDDHA PURUSHA - One who has realized the Supreme Being-
10 NADHAMUNI NARAYANA AYYANGAR – Author's spiritual guru, uncle, for more details Refer- https://www.hramakrishnan.com/myguru.htm
11 ISHTA DEIVAM – Preferred Deity.
12 GAYATRI MANTRA - It is a Sanskrit mantra that has been chanted for thousands of years. It was written down during the Vedic period (1500-500 BCE) and is considered to be one of the oldest known and most powerful mantras. It is said to contain all the knowledge of the universe.

have come from the mouth of the "Parabrahmam[13]". All my experiences are related to Sanathana Dharma[14].

Secondly, I have used many Sanskrit words in this book. These are unique with meanings that were discovered by the ancient rishis and can never be translated into any foreign language. However, I also felt that I should make those understandable, to some extent, to people of other cultures and religions. So, I have made an attempt to translate some of those words.

Although some words have deeper meaning, I have continued to use those as they are popular with the readers. For example, the word "**ANANDA**" has a deeper meaning and can be translated to "ABSOLUTE BLISS". And the word "**TRANSCENDENCE**" can also sometimes refer to a state of the mind where a person has no control. The state that I have mentioned in this book, or the state that I have experienced, actually refers to an "**ELEVATED STATE OF CONSCIOUSNESS**".

And finally, Indian classical music is a child of Sanathana Dharma. It's a Veda of Ragas[15] and Swaras[16]. It's Tantrik[17] in nature. It doesn't exist on its own, its identity is Sanatana Dharma, and its purpose is to experience the "Parabrahmam". It helps us to identify & experience our "ishta-deivam".

It is NOT just an art form, however a medium to connect to our "ishta-deivam". This is because the Sapthaswarams[18] have originated from the mouth of Lord Shiva & so are the Raginis[19].

Every Raga is a "Yogini[20]" for me and I decorate her with flowers & worship her everyday. Sapthaswaras are my mantras

---

13   PARABRAHMAM - Eternal Supreme Reality.
14   SANATHANA DHARMA – HINDUISM.
15   RAGA/RAGAM - A raga is a melodic framework for improvisation in Indian classical music akin to a melodic mode.
16   SWARAS – Notes.
17   TANTRIK - Ritualistic
18   SAPTHASWARA – 7 "SWARAS" i.e., Notes.
19   RAGINI – Indian classical Melody.
20   YOGINI – Power that facilitates the divine union.

and discovering the emotions hidden in these Swaras is my daily Japa[21].

You might wonder what you will get from this memoir.

When you finish reading this memoir, you will realize that the ultimate goal of spiritual practice is not to produce short-lived experiences, but to realize the true divine nature of the Consciousness within us.

If you have just started your spiritual journey, these experiences will motivate you. Because I believe that every moment in our life happens for a reason. Every moment is new, it unfolds itself, takes a spiritually evolved form, and allows us to grow in our spiritual journey. Although most of us are born with a disease called "sandeham[22]", I looked at the cure and that was "asAdhyamAna Nambikkai[23]" in the "Parabrahmam".

If you are an Indian classical musician and deeply interested in spirituality, I can promise you that when you finish reading this memoir, you will start re-discovering your "sangeetha-thwam[24]". And, I strongly believe that a musician is born with either of the 4 "varnas[25]" i.e., wisdom, courage, love & harmony, perfection & meticulousness. I always associate these with the Goddesses Mahatripurasundari, Mahakali, Mahalakshmi & Maha Saraswathi.

Guided by my mama and my music gurus, I identified the 'varna' I was born with and diligently worked on developing the other facets, knowing that to connect with my '"ishta-deivam",' I would require all of these qualities in my music. I discovered this at a very young age and have been enjoying and relishing every moment of my journey. You too will recognize this when you finish reading this memoir.

21	JAPA - Chant
22	SANDEHAM – Doubt.
23	ASADHYAMANA NAMBIKKAI – A very strong belief.
24	SANGEETHA-THWAM - Essence of Music.
25	VARNAS – Colors, Qualities.

I have looked at all the small moments in time, and delved deeper into what happened and what it meant to me. I found meaning in every moment of my life even in the strangest spiritual experiences. And I have attempted to reveal as many experiences as I can through this memoir. As a Sadhak, my connection with my gurus holds a very unique place in my heart.

While there are experiences, conversations, answers to certain questions, and moments of truth that are impossible to share, I have made an effort to recount some cherished moments from my life.

CHAPTER 1

THE BEGINNING

> *"Music is the highest art and, to those who understand is the highest worship"*
> **- Swami Vivekananda**

THE CONCERT

It was a Sunday afternoon in 2008.

I was about to perform a 2.5-hour Carnatic[26] music concert at a cherished "sabha[27]" in Chennai. This Sabha has a rich history of supporting classical music, dance, and theater all year round.

This concert was very important to me because two highly respected Carnatic music legends were going to be in the audience.

The first luminary was the renowned musician from Tamil Nadu and Andhra Pradesh, the late Vidushi[28] Smt. Jayalakshmi Santhanam will refer to her as "VIDUSHI", who was also one of my gurus in my later years. Her music was steeped in profound classicism, and her knowledge of Carnatic music was unparalleled.

The other distinguished figure was the late Prof. TR Subramaniam (TRS), who effortlessly blended populism with the intricate art of Pallavi[29] singing, preserving its complexity and classicism.

Both these stalwarts attentively listened to my concert and graced the stage to felicitate us. Their presence was a great blessing for me.

However, it was the conversation I had with Vidushi after the concert that re-kindled my spiritual desire, and also left an indelible mark on my musical journey.

Vidushi initiated the conversation with a question that initially caught me off guard, "Gayatri, you performed very well, but

---
26   CARNATIC MUSIC - Indian Classical Music Genre.
27   SABHA - Art Organization.
28   VIDUSHI – Female musician who is an expert in Indian classical music..
29   PALLAVI - Generally in a Carnatic music concert, the musician creates a one line in a particular RAGA and TALA of choice and expands it using her improvisational skills

there was something that I have always experienced in your renditions, and that was missing in today's concert. Do you know what that was?"

I knew what she was talking about.

I wanted to change the topic. "Mami[30], didn't I add enough creative elements to my Raga Alapanas[31]? I did add long and short phrases, and also included intricate Brigha[32]

"You did and they were beautiful, you also incorporated your guru Vairamangalam's[33] style in your Swara Prastharams[34], featuring his signature 'kanakku'[35] swaras[36] and sarva laghu[37] patterns," Vidushi replied.

"Mami, are you saying that my Pallavi wasn't good enough?"

"No, TRS liked your Pallavi, it was simple, however had the required grammar, he also praised your thanam[38] It was very powerful."

"And you did include rare compositions, vivadi[39] ragams too, which I liked. And the concluding Abhang[40] was also very powerful," Vidushi continued.

She paused for a while; I asked, "Mami, I'm not sure what I missed."

---

30   MAMI - Means Aunt in Tamil. Calling someone with respect.
31   ALAPANAS – Expanding the RAGA i.e. Melody.
32   BRIGHA - Subtle voice modulations used in Carnatic Music.
33   VAIRAMANGALAM – the author's Music Guru.
34   KALPANA SWARAS - Elaborations of SWARAS.
35   KANAKKU SWARAS – Singing the SWARAS using Mathematical calculations.
36   SWARAS - 7 notes
37   SARVA LAGHU – An improvisational method of building the SWARAS.
38   THANAM – A unique aspect in Carnatic music, it's very beautiful because of two features, the word "ANANDHAM" is elaborated in different ways using a Raga, it focuses on the "LAYA" i.e., Rhythm aspects.
39   VIVADHI – Dissonant notes.
40   ABHANG - Devotional song in Marathi language.

Vidushi replied, "You did a fantastic job in your performance, showcasing creativity and emotion. however, I will never forget the experience I had when I listened to your **Bangaru Kamakshi**[41] once at your house bhajan[42], in the presence of your mama. That magic was missing in all your renditions today. Why didn't you sing "Bangaru Kamakshi", you told me you would, did you forget that?

How can I ever forget that composition? How can I forget that mystical experience?

How many lifetimes OF "Thapas[43]" have I undertaken in my past lives to come under the shadow of a great Sidha Purusha? How can I share that intimate moment with anyone?

---

41   BANGARU KAMAKSHI - Composition of Syama Sastri who was a Carnatic music composer
42   BHAJAN/BHAJANS – A devotional gathering.
43   THAPAS - Based on the root Tap (तप्) meaning "to heat, to give out warmth, to shine, to burn". The term evolves to also mean "to suffer, to mortify the body, undergo penance" in order to "burn away past karma" and liberate oneself.

SIDDHA PURUSHA

The beautiful bhajan room in our house in Triplicane[44] was well-lit and getting ready for the Saturday bhajan. There were many photos & vigrahams[45] of Sanathana Dharma deities.

And for me, the most beautiful vigraham was the cute little Pillayar[46] standing with his "Vel"[47] in his one hand, smilingly waiting to invite the bhakthas[48] who attended the bhajan every Saturday.

Bhajans have been ongoing in this room for many years, and the divine vibrations it imparts can only be felt through personal experience.

My athai[49] and mama were sitting in their respective spots in the bhajan room and getting ready for Saturday's bhajan.

"Where is Gayatri?" Mama asked my athai.

Mama, as I affectionately called him, was a remarkable Yogi[50], a mystic Siddha Purusha, an incredibly humble and down-to-earth individual. I often reflect on the spontaneous chain of events that brought us together, starting with my athai who is my father's elder sister, marrying this enlightened Siddha Purusha and choosing to raise me from the day I was born.

"She is downstairs having her lunch, I'm going down to get fruits, will ask her to get ready for the bhajan," said my athai.

---

44   TRIPLICANE – A suburb in Chennai, Tamil Nadu, India.
45   VIGRAHAM – Idols.
46   PILLAYAR – Referring to Lord Ganesha in Tamil.
47   VEL – Spear. Specially manifested by H.H. Nadhamuni Narayana Ayyangar for devotees & disciples.
48   BHAKTHA – Devotees of BHAGAWAN i.e. The Eternal Supreme.
49   ATHAI – Aunt in Tamil.
50   YOGI - A practitioner of Yoga, including a sannyasin or practitioner of meditation in Indian religions

"Tomorrow, you have Vairamangalam class, did you practice the "Vanajasana[51]" composition that he taught you last week?" I could also hear my father's[52] voice.

My very first music guru was my father, who began training me when I was just three years old. I was also fortunate to accompany him to the music classes of the eminent Carnatic stalwart, Sangitha Kalanidhi[53] PROF. S. Ramanathan. My father is a great musician, and during my formative years, his music and renditions were a tremendous source of inspiration for me.

Through him, I found my second and most important musical guru who gave me the classics that I enjoy today, my music guru Kalaimamani[54]. Late. Vairamangalam Lakshminarayanan. I cherish those seventeen years of my glorious musical life with him. He was a stalwart however, a very simple man, exceptionally talented in all aspects of Carnatic music. His outpourings of manodharma[55] during my class sessions were unimaginable; however, he was a very down-to-earth humble musician, a very kind & affectionate guru who was always ready to share his ocean of knowledge with me and a strict teacher too.

"I heard you practicing **Bangaru Kamakshi** this morning in the bhajan room, did you practice for tomorrow's class?" my father asked again.

I was fully aware of what was going on around me. However, I had no interest in anything.

"Is the sAthumdhu[56] nice? Why are you always lost in your world? Appa[57] is asking you, why don't you answer" asked my

---

51   VANAJASANA – A composition of Carnatic Music composer Subbaraya Sastri who lived in the 18th century.
52   FATHER – Author's Father S. Lakshminarasimhan, is a great vocalist as well as a harmonium artist, who was trained in Hindustani music, "Namasankeerthanam" as well as Carnatic music.
53   SANGITHA KALANIDHI - An award given to a musician.
54   KALAIMAMANI - An award given to a musician.
55   MANODHARMA – Improvisations.
56   SATHUMDHU - Tomato soup.
57   APPA – Father in Tamil.

mother. "yaar thalailo enna mazhai pozhinzha madiri irukkiye eppayum[58]" she continued...

I heard her voice too; however, I was eating for the sake of eating..

I had been in a very unique blissful state since the morning. I was present however not in this world, I never wanted to come out of that state.

It was a state of ecstasy, wanting to escape the bounds of this material world forever, break free from my limitations, and reach that supreme reality. All mental activities came to a complete stop that morning. It was a state of inner freedom, being utterly free from the problems and limitations of this body and mind, it was a state that transcended all my sufferings, limitations, and imperfections.

If my mama hadn't entered the bhajan room that morning, if he hadn't touched the top of my head while I was singing the line **'Bangaru Kamakshi'** in the raga Varali, I wouldn't have experienced the divine transcendental state, nor would I have known what the highest state of ecstasy could be.

The experience that surged within me at that very instant is beyond the reach of any language. There simply exists no words to adequately capture that profound experience.

As the SHASTRAS[59] say the experiences are "ANIRVACHANEEYAM[60], my attempt to put that experience into words can only capture SO MUCH AND NO MORE.

As Jagathguru Adi Shankaracharya[61] says in his Soundarya Lahari[62] "An ocean of beauty". I could feel the silence, and smell

---

58   YAAR THALAIYILO ENNA MAZHAI – It's a colloquial way of saying in Tamil that the person is lost in her own world.
59   SHASTRAS - Hindu sacred scriptures
60   ANIRVACHANEEYAM - That which can never be described.
61   JAGATHGURU ADI SHANKARACHARYA - 8th-century Indian Vedic scholar and teacher (acharya).
62   SOUNDARYA LAHARI - famous literary work in Sanskrit attributed to Pushpadanta as well as Adi Shankaracharya

her fragrance, there was so much glow on her face, and her most compassionate beautiful eyes were in partial bloom.

"I can't help but wonder about the good karma from my past lives that led me to be guided by my mama. He was as compassionate as the divine mother.

The experiences I had while growing up under him are beyond words.

He was the one who nurtured my music in such a mystic way that my renditions became the medium for me to connect with my "ishta-deivam". Whenever the disciples walked in to get my mama's blessings, and if they were going through any health issues or stressful situations in their life, he would make me sing for them. The actual magic lay in the mystic music that he nurtured in me, he was a great Siddha Purusha and my music was fortunate to be his chosen medium.

From this incident onwards, my music helped me to quickly go into that magical transcendental state of pure bliss and experience that divine longing; I could instantly connect with my "ishta-deivam" through my music.

The mystical experience that yogis generally get after years of meditation, detachment, renunciation, and mindfulness, was very easily made available to me through my music, and it was generously gifted to me by my mama.

I was not lost; I was totally immersed in the flow of experience and the "I" didn't exist. I continued to be in that spiritual divine state for many years and all I wished was to be in that state all the time.

Every cell in my body kept longing for that state of ecstasy.

How can I describe that "anubhoothi[63]"?

---

63   ANUBHOOTHI - Refers to profound spiritual experiences, often depicted in literature and art, such as the transcendent love between Goddess Valli and Lord Murugan.

CHAPTER 2

TRANSCENDENT

सरस्वत्या लक्ष्म्या विधिहरिसपत्नो विहरते
रतेः पातिव्रत्यं शिथिलयति रम्येण वपुषा ।
चिरं जीवन्नेव क्षपितपशुपाशव्यतिकरः
परानन्दाभिख्यम् रसयति रसं त्वद्भजनवान् ॥ ९९॥

Those who worship thee, oh mother, are so learned and so rich, that even Brahma and Vishnu, are jealous of them. They are so handsome that even the wife of Cupid, Rathi, yearns for them.
He is unbound from the ties of this birth, always enjoys ecstatic happiness, and lives forever.
- Soundarya Lahari
- Jagadguru Sri. Adi Shankaracharya

THE FIRST "ANUBHOOTHI"

"Gayatri, mama is calling you, eat soon and go upstairs" I could feel the cold air coming from the fridge, athai had opened it to take out the fruits for the bhajan.

"Wear those gold earrings that I bought for you, why don't you have any interest in all these things," she continued,

How can I look at all these worldly items?

Can these supposedly beautiful gold ornaments come even close to those brilliant eyes that are beyond all those most beautiful things that one could ever imagine?

However, having said that, without my athai, I might never have had the extraordinary privilege of growing up in the radiant presence of a Yogi.

In the words of Goddess Andal, "Yetraikkum Yezhezh Piravikkum[64]", I find myself eternally indebted to my athai for not just constantly showering her love and affection on me but for also granting me the priceless gift of allowing me to grow under a Sidha Purusha.

"At least wear a good dress for the bhajan not the same old dress, don't forget the dupatta[65]" she continued. I didn't respond. I cleaned my plate and was about to go upstairs, when Babu Mama came out from his kitchen, waiting to ask me.

"Gayatri, can you please sing the "neene dhoddavano[66]" Today for the bhajan" asked Babu Mama.

---

64   YEZHEZH PIRAVIKKUM – GODDESS ANDAL's "Thiruppavai" which is a set of special 30 verses written by her in praise of Lord Krishna.
65   DUPATTA - Indian scarf
66   NEENE DODDAVANO - A composition of a composer in the name PURANDHARA DASA who has written many devotional songs on many Hindu gods and goddesses.

My mama had many disciples, and one of them was this wonderful couple who lived in our family's outhouse. I affectionately called the gentleman "Babu Mama" and his wife "Bathai."

"Please don't ask her to sing that song, she will once again start the same old story, that you attended her competition," athai said to Babu mama.

It was not a story, I did see him sitting in the third row, why should I make it up, then I thought to myself, I am living with my mama who is not an ordinary man however a Yogi. These mystic things are quite normal to me.

Babu Mama had a deep appreciation for my music and would often attend all my competitions, taking a seat in the audience to enjoy my renditions. He had intended to be present for this particular competition as well, which happened a week before, however unfortunately, work commitments compelled him to leave the city two days before the event.

I was aware of his absence.

On that day, I took the stage to sing "Neene Dhoddavno" in the Ragam Revathi, I made a small slip in pronunciation, and said "thwarathi" instead of "dharathi." Nevertheless, I managed to deliver a strong performance.

To my surprise, I spotted Babu Mama in the audience, seated on the third row, thoroughly enjoying my music, and eagerly awaiting the moment to applaud.

After my performance, I had to be with the other students for a while. However, when I learnt that I had won the first prize, I was eager to greet my Babu Mama. Rushing to the third row, I discovered he had already left. I felt a mix of happiness and confusion.

Upon returning home, my athai, amma[67] & patti [68] celebrated my victory, however, they laughed at me when I insisted that "Babu Mama" had been in the audience.

No one believed me, unfortunately.

"Gayatri, since morning mama has been in the bhajan room, many disciples have been coming today, so don't go to that room now, you can show him your medal after everyone has left," athai said

"No athai I want to go now," I replied.

"Fine, then take these coffee tumblers along," she said.

I went in with the coffee tumblers and medal on my neck, gave the coffee to everyone, sought mama's blessings, and showed him my medal.

Mama smiled and said, "Why didn't you pronounce it correctly? Weren't you supposed to say "Dharathi"?. Narasimha broke open the pillar and emerged fast. Next time you sing, focus on the pronunciations."

I wasn't surprised, if mama wanted, he would exist anywhere. And if I wanted to, he would exist there.

If just a few hours with a Siddha Purusha can offer one an unimaginable experience, think about what twenty-five growing years of my life with him have been like!

Countless similar incidents from those remarkable twenty-five years lie waiting to be explored, to say I was fortunate would be an understatement.

The Vidushi was correct; it's impossible for my music to not have the mystic magic when my mama was the one who nurtured my music all those years.

---

67   AMMA – Mother in Tamil.
68   PATTI – Grandma in Tamil.

The role of my mama was to guide and assist me in removing obstacles along my spiritual journey and initiate me into the spiritual process. Bestowing that "Anubhoothi" upon me was simply part of that process.

Climbing the divine spiritual mountain isn't easy, as one has to take eighty-four lakhs of difficult, tough steps. This number reminds me of akka Mahadevi's[69] vachana[70], "enbathu nangu laksha yoni yolage bandhe."

However, unlike everyone, I never had to climb these, I was fortunate to have that special pushpaka vimanam[71] readily waiting for me, I'd say it was my mama's siddhi that he blessed me with. However he didn't stop there, after reaching the top of the mountain, like how an affectionate father will carefully take his daughter's hands and keep on the groom's hand, mama took my hands and kept them on the feet of the ever-eternal supreme Parashakthi[72], without whom none of these universes exists, without her no spiritual union is possible, without her one can never ever experience the "ishta-deivam". And she has been waiting to take me to that special universe of divine experiences, it was an experience that can't be described in words.

It was an ecstasy of happiness, ecstasy of separation, ecstasy exhibited before meeting my "ishta-deivam", and it was also a state of divine union, a state of divine love anxieties. I was also afraid of being separated from my "ishta-deivam"'s beautiful eyes and smile.

How can I ever imagine that ecstatic experience without the blessings of a Sidha Purusha?

---

69   AKKA MAHADEVI – A great mystic women saint of Karnataka, India, who lived in the 11th century.
70   VACHANA - Composition in Kannada.
71   PUSHPAKA VIMANAM - Divine vehicle.
72   PARASHAKTHI – The Eternal Supreme Goddess.

How fortunate I was. I was in this state of ecstasy for many years and that was only possible because of his constant physical presence & his compassionate grace on me.

Mystic experiences create an opportunity for us to discover what the great rishis have discovered and when we realize that our central nature is to be eternal, pure, and divine, all our sufferings come to an end.

However, going beyond these experiences can only lead us to Moksha. These experiences are important however I later realized that enlightenment has to be the goal and I must bear the primary responsibility for my own "ATMA SAKSHATKARA" i.e. Self-Realization.

Later in my life, when I experienced extremely difficult life situations, I discovered this.

Just as curd transforms into butter and then into ghee through the process of churning. The vigorous churning started happening in my life too. It began with the loss of my mama's physical presence and it was not something that I was ready for.

It was 2003, I still remember that moment of deep grief, crying alone in that new 3-bedroom apartment in a country where women were not allowed to walk on streets without their "abhaya".

My lonely cry was indeed loud however I could still hear his voice, him singing his all-time favorite Janabai's[73] Abhang "vitumazha lenkurawala". It was strong, divine, and healing.

However Sidha Purushas don't go away. My mama disappeared only for a short while.

The mystic magic that he nurtured in my music stayed with me, his pushpaka vimanam also stayed with me, however, did Parashakthi stay with me?

The next phase of my life began.

---

73   JANABAI – A Mystic woman saint of Maharashtra who lived in the 13th century. She has written many ABHANGS.

Gayatri's Carnatic Music Guru

Vidwan. S. Laksminarasimhan

Vidwan. Prof. S. Ramanathan

Vidushi. Jayalakshmi Santhanam

Vidwan. Vairamangalam Lakshminarayanan

Vidushi. Meena Subramaniam

CHAPTER 3

LIFE UNFOLDS

> *"The utterance of sound without knowledge of the {true} import bears no fruit, {even as} the offering thrown over ashes in the absence of fire does not burst into flame"*
> **- Varivasya-Rahasya Sri Bhaskararaya Makhin**[74]

---

74   BHASKARA RAYA – 16th century religious exponent and writer best known for his contributions to the "SHAKTHA" (Denomination where PARASHAKTHI is worshiped as the Supreme deity) tradition of Hinduism.

KALI – GODDESS OF TIME & CHANGE

"The purpose of "manodharma[75]" lies in bringing out the concealed divinity within the Ragini and compositions, rather than in using them to display one's skills in pursuit of fame and material pleasures."

"I will never forget the experience I had when I listened to your **Bangaru Kamakshi** once at your house bhajan, in the presence of your mama. That magic was missing in all your renditions today. Why?" Vidushi asked.

I couldn't say anything.

There is a very fine border between this conceptual impermanent world & concept-free ultimate reality of Pure Consciousness which is the only truth and is beyond "DESHA, KALA, VASTHU" i.e. "Place, Time & Object."

Although I had lost my mama's physical presence, I knew how to traverse between these two spaces through my music. I had the ability to take myself to that concept-free ultimate reality through my own music and travel back to this conceptual world. I always had the pushpaka vimana waiting for me. That was never an issue.

For some years, I chose to not "let-go".

I knew that I must live in this material world, I had to do my duties. I have a family to look after, I have responsibilities in this life and my music must not exist for my own experiences. These were some excuses that I gave to myself.

And to appear "sane," I told myself that I have to be "present" in this conceptual world. Being Sane or Insane are just lines that we create for ourselves. And we do cross them sometimes.

What is sane for you might be insane for me. As Swami Ramakrishna Paramahamsa says, all of us are mad at something.

---

75   MANODHARMA – Improvisations.

So, to appear "sane" I stopped myself from going into that transcendental state. And to implement this, I started using more of the manodharma elements that were available in our Indian classical music. This was to activate the logical part of my brain.

Is this even possible? Certain aspects of manodharma helped me stay grounded in this material world because I thought that they were "abstract"[76]. Abstract generally refers to anything that exists in thought or as an idea but not having a physical or concrete existence.

When my Bhakthi[77] evolved, I started seeing the Yoginis through every Raga. I started experiencing the divine existence of the Yogini as Raginis. I realized my mistake, and this was when every Yogini started helping me in my spiritual journey. This wouldn't have been possible without my mama's blessings.

Until a certain point in my life, I didn't understand the importance of the gift that I was blessed with. And generally, when difficult situations come into our life, we start looking inwards. And that's when I realized how fortunate I was.

The first major life situation that happened, which I call the "baby lock up[78]" incident realigned my vision.

To me, Bhakthi has always been like the ever-glowing sun. Like how nobody can hide the brightness of the sun, my Bhakthi was unaffected. Although the "baby lock up" incident impacted us, my Bhakthi for my "ishta-deivam" only grew stronger.

76	ABSTRACT – Generally, an alapana (improvisation of a Raga) is defined as an abstract essay of Raga.
77	BHAKTHI – A path of devotion. Devotion here refers to NOT towards material objects however only to BHAGWAN. i.e. The Eternal Supreme.
78	BABY-LOCKUP - Once when the author went early to pick up her 12 month old daughter from a daycare, she was shocked to find the center staff had irresponsibly locked the center and left, leaving the baby alone locked up inside and in a bassinet. Miraculously, the baby survived.

The conversation with vidushi reminded me that I am one of those fortunate ones and I should let myself go.

That's when I decided that I would take myself back to that state of ecstasy through my music. I was now ready for that big jump.

I jumped on that boat and re-started my journey; I was looking forward to all the good, great & mystical experiences that my "ishta-deivam" was waiting to give me. Isn't the purpose of this life "Saranagathi[79]"?

I came back from my concert, changed into my normal clothes, went into my bhajan room, turned my tanpura[80] on, started singing the virutham "un irupuram idam kondavar thaduthanaro, Ma Shakthi Thay ennai[81]"

Her eyes were beautiful however Red. Oh no, she was not my Parashakthi, she was darkest of dark, covered in blood, her smile was indeed beautiful, she was not guiding me, my heart experienced intense bliss and also a fear of death, how can I experience both, she did not take me on her hands, she pushed me away, and suddenly I see nothing, my vision came to an end. Tears flowed from my eyes; I was in deepest sorrow.

"Hema?[82] Why did Gayatri suddenly stop singing?" asked my athai, while busy cutting the vegetables in the downstairs kitchen.

"I don't know, maybe she is talking to someone, you don't go up, akka[83], your legs will hurt." I could hear my amma's voice.

"It's okay, she hasn't eaten anything since this morning, let me go and check." My athai walked up to the bhajan room.

79 SARANAGATI - Complete surrender.
80 TANPURA - Indian Musical instrument
81 VIRUTHAM – This was written by the author's grandfather Kumarmangalam Srinivasaraghavan, a great composer, with more than 500 compositions to his credit.
82 HEMA – Author's mother's name.
83 AKKA – Elder sister / Sister in law in Tamil.

"Gayatri, Gayatri, what happened, wake up" I could hear my athai's voice.

I realized that I had come back to this conceptual world with great disappointment and sorrow. Parashakthi, why did you do this to me, why are you angry with me?

"You have a concert at Kapaleeswarar[84] temple tomorrow, you are not well I will call Auto Mama[85] and cancel the concert," my athai said

Although I could hear Athai's voice, she appeared unreal to me.

The word Auto Mama stuck with me. He was a popular newscaster, a great Carnatic musician, a konakkol[86] artist, a journalist & an ardent disciple of my mama. I called him "auto mama" affectionately, because he used to come to our house for Saturday bhajans in his auto, he was one of my favorite uncles and taught me the deepest meaning of the Guru Bhakthi.

The Bhakthi he had for his guru was unimaginable. He is the one, who is very dear to me, whom I adore, respect, admire & I have learnt a lot of life lessons from him. Athai's mention of "Auto mama" reminded me of his strongest Guru Bhakthi.

Oh no, how did I forget my mama who is my first guru? I know I have his blessings; however I took him for granted, was I arrogant? I couldn't stop crying.

That night's dream was a great beginning.

---

84 KAPALEESWARAR - A temple in Chennai, Tamil Nadu.
85 AUTO MAMA – He was a popular newscaster, a great Carnatic musician, a konnakol artist & a journalist.
86 KONNAKKOL - Art of performing percussion syllables vocally.

FIRE

I went into the room where Mama was lying on his bed, after that big stroke, he was fully bedridden. Athai was cleaning up the room and removing his diapers. She left the room. I sat next to his bed. He always used to touch my nose if he wanted to say something and as always, he touched my nose. He had lost his ability to talk, however, I could hear the word "Thapas" coming from his mouth.

"Gayatri, wake up, you have the pradosham[87] concert at Kapaleeswarar today, don't you remember?"

It was five in the morning. I woke up and realized that Mama had come into my dream.

What did he mean by "Thapas"?

I did some quick practice after having my lunch and then I started getting ready for the concert.

While I was wearing my saree, my mind was constantly thinking about the word "Thapas". I had no idea what it was.

A thought came to me, how can Parashakthi not bless me tonight? It's going to be her "kshetram[88]".

However, what about the audience? I was convinced that my "anubhoothi" is more important to me and that is all I want from now on.

There was a good crowd at Kapaleeswarar temple, I finished singing the composition "Kana kankodi vendum[89]" in the ragam Kamboji. After finishing the Kalpana swarams[90], I decid-

---

87   PRADOSHAM - Special day for Lord Shiva.
88   KSHETRAM – A divine place, Temple.
89   KANA KAN – A composition of Carnatic music composer Papanasam Sivan who lived in the 19th century.
90   MANODHARMA - Improvising the notes.

ed to take up the composition "kamakoti peetavasini[91]" as the main item and I had a strong reason for this.

After a detailed elaboration of Ragam simhendramadhyamam, I started singing the composition, when I moved on to do the nereval[92] for the lines "Nadha Bindu Kala Swaroopini[93]" I decided to "let go".

I consciously allowed myself to immerse in those lines. I didn't care about the crowd, the concert, or my supporting artists, I didn't want anything at that moment.

My desire for enlightenment grew stronger.

Although people were sitting all round. I didn't hesitate; everything was insignificant to me. A child's mother would want her child to stop playing and start eating, however the child will never want to. He is so much into that game that he/she is neither hungry nor thinking about anything, I was exactly in this state, I allowed myself to let go.

All I wanted at that time was to experience Parashakthi's compassion, I desperately wanted to experience once again that same state of happiness, the ecstasy of separation, ecstasy exhibited before meeting my "ishta-deivam", that state of divine union. I let go.

And Parashakthi was kind enough to take me on her hands this time, why wouldn't she? She lives in these lines "nadha bindu kala swaroopini".

And I did hear the violinist, and I could see him looking puzzled at my father, I could see the mridangist[94] looking at the violinist unaware of what to do, his sarva laghu continued with no intention.

---

91   KAMAKOTI PEETAVASINI A composition of carnatic music composer Muthuswamy Dikshitar who lived in the 18th century.
92   NEREVAL - Improvising the lines of a composition in Carnatic music.
93   NADHA BINDU KALA SWAROOPINI - A line from the composition "KAMAKOTI" of Muthuswami Dikshitar.
94   MRIDANGAM – Percussionist.

I was completely aware of everything around me.

I was overjoyed, Parashakthi's hands waiting to give me, I had no fear this time, her eyes were indeed beautiful, and she smiled, however then everything stopped suddenly, I lost her, I saw nothing now, my vision came to an end. Why would she refuse to give me what I wanted, what I longed for, how can she be so unkind to me, why did she do this. Tears flowed from my eyes, once again I was in deepest sorrow.

I could feel the hands of my father from behind, quickly finished the nereval, Kalpana swarams, and finally the concert.

Many from the audience came to me, and expressed their happiness and I could hear a lady telling me "kannu munnadi konduvandutta, Ambalai[95]".

That Ambal[96] was not kind to me. Why?

"Why did you stop in the middle of the nereval?" Auto Mama asked me while getting into the car.

How can I tell him that I made that choice of letting go?

How can I tell him that I wanted that state of a divine union that I have been longing for?

How can I tell him that I have been struggling to re-experience that intimate moment that I was sharing with my "ishta-deivam" and Parashakthi refused to help me for the second time?

Do I even have words to describe my agony, my pain, my suffering?

I stayed silent. He smiled and left.

However, questions started pouring in; Did I lose my Parashakthi's grace forever? Will I ever get it back? What mistakes did I make? In this lifetime or past? Did I take my mama's blessings

---

[95] KANNU MUNNADI KONDUVANDHUTTA – "You brought AMBAL before my eyes" in Tamil.
[96] AMBAL – Goddess Kalpagambikai.

for granted? Why should I sing for others? What is the purpose of my life?

For the first time, I felt completely helpless and alone.

I was unable to understand her LEELA[97]. I didn't have the patience.

I thought that I had done enough Bhakthi to be entitled to all her blessings, all possible experiences. How arrogant I was. I didn't realize that I had a very long way to go.

"Sridhar, call your driver, I want to go home," Athai asked her cousin.

Sridhar, whom I affectionately call "Kuttimama", is a well-known yoga guru, senior teacher of the Krishnamachariya yoga mandiram, and a direct disciple of the legendary Yoga Guru TKV Desikachar.

We got into the car. Kuttimama took my hands, why would he check my pulse? I'm absolutely fine, I thought.

"Gayatri, kutcheri[98] was very nice, you sang very well. Did you do the pranayama[99] this morning?" I nodded.

He continued, but the yoga terms that he was talking about never reached my ears.

I was happy, because, unlike others, he didn't ask me what happened, he seemed to have understood everything. Why wouldn't he, he is a great yoga guru.

"Did the kutcheri go well?" my patti asked my appa, while my athai & I were getting out of the car.

---

97   LEELA – Loosely translated as "pastime". however it is not the material world's recreational activities.
98   KUTCHERI – Concert.
99   PRANAYAMA - Pranayama is the practice of breath regulation

"Eppa paru amma thaye naan oru yezahi enakku yaravudhu pichai podungolenu azhardhuku than iva pirandirukka[100]" and everyone laughed.

Appa was referring to a particular virutham[101] in praise of Lord Muruga that I sang in that concert. Me detaching myself from this world while singing, is not something that he has liked.

I didn't say anything, however I enjoyed his sense of humor. I went into the kitchen to eat something,

My amma was sitting on the floor and kneading the flour. "Take this, put it on a pan," she told me.

"It is NOT clean, clean it first." I cleaned it, and put it on the stove.

"can't you see the fire isn't on, turn it on," she said.

That struck me. Both the Pan & the Fire are needed to make a roti[102].

It is not enough if I know how to make roti, my Pan is supposed to be clean & I should turn the fire on.

Am I clean? Shouldn't I first get rid of all my worldly desires, greed, jealousy, fear, hatred & anger?

I turned the fire on. And my Thapas began.

---

100   VIRUTHAM – This was written by author's grandfather Kumarmangalam Srinivasaraghavan, a great composer, with more than 500 compositions to his credit.
101   VIRUTHAM - Poem
102   Roti - Indian bread

CHAPTER 4

INTENSE THAPAS

> *"All Ego gone, Living as THAT alone is THAPAS"*
> **- Sri Ramana Maharshi**

CONSCIOUSNESS

"Mr. Iyengar,[103] her pulse is normal; however she has lost Consciousness, we will have to take her to the emergency room." I could hear the paramedic's voice. It was a bright Sunday afternoon in the suburbs of Michigan.

THIS IS a JOKE!

How can I lose "Consciousness" when I hear the voice of these paramedics, my husband's voice, my daughter's voice, the sound of the ambulance, the sound of them banging on my doors, and I can also feel my husband's touch, paramedics touching me.

"Gayatri, I'm Dr. Sharp. Do you know where you are?"

Of course, I knew.

I opened my eyes.

What an experience it was, continuous tears flowing from my eyes while I was singing the lines of Goddess Andal's "Matrai Nam kamangal Matrelo Yempavai[104]".

Dr. Sharp wouldn't understand if I told him that I'm very much conscious and my Consciousness is never changing, it's limitless, transcendental, utterly unaffected by anything.

If I didn't lose my "Consciousness", why was my "physical body" in this hospital?

What this doctor can actually see is my physical body. He doesn't know if anything existed beyond this.

What he can see is my "Annamaya Kosha" i.e., food sheath. This physical body is made of matter, which includes the skin, bones, muscles, organs, and other tissues.

---

103   IYENGAR – the author's husband's last name.
104   MATRAI NAM KAMANGAL MATRELO YEMPAVAI - Get rid of all my worldly desires.

My brain is a physical object for him but not my mind, intellect, thoughts, memories, emotions, and senses. All these are part of my subtle body, which is not tangible, can't be seen, heard, smelled, touched, or tasted by him.

My tanpura is a physical object. The happiness that I get when I turn it on is subtle.

Another body that this doctor is not aware of is "Karana Shareeram", which is the cause for both my physical & subtle body.

If I break the seed of a mango, I can't see anything. All the qualities of the mango are hidden in it, the seed is the cause for the mango.

In the same way, my causal body existed in an encoded form even before this "Shrishti[105]" even before the "Pralayam[106]" & is the cause for all my rebirths.

And out of this causal body, a subtle body came out, and every time I took birth, a physical body came out. This will continue to exist as long as I have spiritual ignorance (Self-Ignorance). It will cease to exist when I get spiritual enlightenment.

When I'm awake, I have all my three bodies, and I use the sun and moonlight to see everything. And this is one of the states of the mind.

When I'm in my dream state, my mind plays back whatever it has recorded so far and some of the experiences in this birth or past get activated in this state. I may not be aware of my physical body but I am identified with my subtle body and I use my own internal light. This is another state of mind.

When I'm enjoying my deep sleep state, there is no mind, intellect, memory, or ego. These are all in unmanifested forms. And in this state my causal body is prominent and so "I" is identi-

---

105   SHRISHTI – Evolution.
106   PRALAYAM – Dissolution.

fied with my causal body. My life forces are functioning in this state, and I'm beyond my physical and subtle bodies.

And with this causal body, "I" traveled into a deeper state, "I" traveled from happy to happier to the happiest state. And I was able to penetrate into the "Anandamaya Kosha" i.e., the blissful sheath, which was actually a reflection of me, the true nature of the Consciousness, that was the truth, the beauty, and the absolute bliss. And in this state, I had nothing to hold on to anymore. I was not aware of the body or my mind, and yet I have NOT fallen asleep there was absolutely no thinking nor thoughts. When I came back from that state, the mind looked back and saw that I existed as awareness itself even without the mind.

A state is something that comes and goes, not the Consciousness. And this Consciousness is "me" which is beyond everything. I can't describe this; it can only be experienced.

Once I can feel that I'm outside this physical & subtle body, there's no mind, because the mind gives me the feeling that I'm inside this body . When I'm outside this body there is no mind and this exactly is transcendence. I can move in the body, move in the mind, move out of the body, move out of the mind, yet I am beyond inside and outside. However, this experience stays with me forever and I have recognized my true self as "Sat-Chit-Ananda[107]".

From the hospital's window, I looked at the moonlight, it was bright as always.

It was not part of the moon, it was independent, pervaded, not limited by the boundary of the moon, and will continue even if the moon disappears. This exactly is my Consciousness, it is not part of this body, it is invisible, it is independent, not limited to the boundaries of this body, and will continue to

---

[107] SAT-CHIT-ANANDA - Sat: truth, absolute being or existence-- that which is enduring and unchanging
Chit: consciousness, understanding and comprehension, Ananda: bliss, a state of pure happiness, joy and sensual pleasure

survive even when this body disappears and after death, it is not available for transaction, because the medium of the transaction has become absent. This is my true nature and this is unworldly.

Well, medical science is just physical science! And believes only in tangible and observable phenomena.

These are beyond the medical science's understanding.

Did Parashakthi help me this time?

BHAVA AAVESHAM[108]

Did my Parashakthi help me?

She made me practice **self-discipline** to accumulate more spiritual merits.

She made me work hard to get rid of my eight enemies: **desires, anger, greed, delusion, jealousy, pride, fear & hatred.**

She made me do the Thapas i.e., **rigorous** musical sadhana for many hours every day.

She made me do "**Namajapam**[109]" of certain "Mantras" continuously for many years.

She made me listen to the discourses of great scholars, of great Bhagavatha[110], for many hours regularly.

She made me interact with great mahatma[111] and enlightened gurus and yogis.

She made me realize that I have to keep nurturing and strengthening myself to that point when I'm ready to penetrate the barriers that confine me within this physical body and finally merge in blissful union with my "ishta-deivam".

Why wouldn't she help me, she did This time in a different way.

She didn't fully walk me through it, maybe she expected me to walk it on my own, I'm not a baby anymore?

So, what happened?

I started consciously traveling beyond the horizon of anyone's imagination to seek my dearest GODDESS ANDAL who had actually possessed me.

---

108   BHAVA AAVESHAM – "Bhava" refers to a state of Consciousness. Refer to SRI RUPA GOSWAMI's magnum opus "Bhakthi-Rasa-Amrita-Sindhu".
109   NAMAJAPAM - Chanting the Mantras.
110   BHAGAVATHA – Devotees.
111   MAHATMA - Great Atmas.

I moved and traveled in my Andal's world, and at the same time, I resided in my own Consciousness.

I was absolutely fully aware of that mystical terrain. I also found that in that terrain nothing was excluded – neither pain nor ecstasy.

I have to admit here that it could be a little death, but I wanted more, my longing for that divine union was howling inside me.

I cut was off from this outside world. It was beyond the span of my mind, it was a state where the mind had taken rise in mind-lessness, a complete thought-free state. There were no limitations of being here. It was absolutely full. Isn't "Anandham[112]" my birthright? Why shouldn't I be adamant?

Bharat[113] was sitting next to me in the Henry Ford hospital, holding my hands. "Dr. Sharp said we can go home, shall we?" he asked.

He has always been a pillar of strength and a tremendous source of emotional support in my life. I feel incredibly fortunate to have him.

I always believed that my mama would only do good for me, I was reminded of that day when I walked into his room. "Mama, which one do you like?" kept the photos of three men next to him, while he was on his bed after that big stroke. He moved his hands slowly and touched the photo of a tall, fair-complexioned, good-looking young man. The name "Bharat" was written on the back of the photo.

I tried moving my left leg, however I couldn't.

I was witness to everything, I was fully aware of what happened, and my mind stopped, but not the Consciousness. I am a pool of Consciousness, it was limitless like space, vast, it was a state where I lost my "i".

---

112   ANANDHAM – Bliss in its fullest.
113   BHARAT – the author's husband.

It will be a waste of my time if I try to explain these things to this doctor.

"Bhava aavesham" is a state, and I can't describe it, it's not a tangible, not an observable phenomenon that medical practitioners believe in.

What I go through every minute is a very passionate, deep, intense, and inseparable absorption in my ishta-deivam. And I call this pain "PARAMA VIRAHA"[114].

For a devotee like me, who is submerged in this state of "PARAMA VIRAHA", experiencing the ishta-deivam in a transcendent state is the only medicine.

Like how medicine can also create side effects in our physical body. This particular medicine that I absorb to experience my ishta-deivam through my music also creates side effects and sometimes an imbalance in the physical body. But at a deeper level, my karma is also a reason for this occasional imbalance.

Do I give up my Bhakthi to have a comfortable worldly life?

I wouldn't be able to. Because, every cell in my body is longing for the divine union with my ishta-deivam. To me, every emotion towards my ishta-deivam is a RASA[115].

Every individual's state of Bhakthi is in a different level of hierarchy. It depends on which phase of the spiritual journey the individual is in. It can be in the beginning stage and can do "VAIDHI" Bhakthi as per the "VIDHI"[116].

Passionate Atma in its advanced stage, is beyond the laws of "VIDHI" and its bhakthi derives from its inner selves. And so, the ultimate goal is also based on this hierarchy.

---

114   PARAMA VIRAHA - to feel a severe pang of separation for my Ishta-deivam.
115   RASA – Can be loosely translated to "taste". However, here, the experience has to be understood in a spiritual context as it is transcendental. It is not the same as the taste we get from a physical object i.e. fruits
116   VIDHI – Convention.

I have finally realized that I have taken enough births in my past and my ultimate goal is only to attain "MOKSHA".

A color-blind person can't understand the color of a crow or apple or lotus or rainbow. They are all the same for him. A 5-year-old girl who has not attained puberty can never understand the labor pain.

My pain of "PARAMA VIRAHA" can only be understood by a fellow SAdhakA who experiences the same.

And for medical practitioners only four states exist– fully aware & aroused, deep sleep, neither aware nor aroused & the fourth state that they normally put everyone under is a state that they categorize as aroused and fully unaware.

I was in a transcendental state that was completely beyond all these.

I was in the highest state of Arousal and in the highest state of Awareness, it was a refined state of my wakefulness, and I entered into the Consciousness of myself.

It was neither turned inwards like the dream state, not turned extroverted like the awake state, nor was it in between, nor was it absent. Was it dark like the deep sleep state? No, it was beyond that, it was dense and deepest and I felt that this state always existed.

This doctor will dismiss this as a mere dream.

Why bother? Let me go home and continue my Thapas.

Even though I entered into the transcendental state, there was a deep desire for that sacred union and that consumed me like a fire, and I became blind, or perhaps a different eye opened, I don't know.

What I actually wanted was to experience that RASA again. That sweet RASA of transcendental love that I experienced when I was twelve. And the one & only Parashakthi can help me. Why didn't she walk me through?

There was a reason. This time, she wanted me to approach and take shelter of the Acharya (Guru) with all sincerity. Did I?

SEVA[117] THROUGH MUSIC

Hold me tightly and lift your left leg." My brother had come from Seattle to help me with my walking; he is also a great cook. He gave me simple walking therapy sessions, cooked tasty food for me, and made every effort to help me walk. By the end of the fifth week, I was able to start walking.

"Do not sing until you have fully recovered, take care." My brother left for Seattle.

"Thanks, Vatsa[118], for your support." Bharat sent him off.

How can I live without singing? All I wanted was Parashakthi's hands. Emotions don't threaten me anymore. I started accepting reality.

Both rice and roti will eliminate hunger. It doesn't matter which one you like. I like roti and that's music for me.

I was about to turn my tanpura on. Notification sounds from my phone distracted me.

It was a YouTube Comment for the thiruppavai[119] that I uploaded two weeks ago, "Madam, thanks for sharing your thiruppavai, I listened to your pasuram[120] every day, I got my health back, thank you very much, Mam"

Another notification sound, this time it was Christina's email –

"Good morning, Gayatri, we are so grateful for the service you provided to our patients and guests and you will certainly be missed as a great asset to our patient healing experience and a person who is more than a joy to interact with. We will share your email and departing notes with the nurse unit leaders so

---

117   SEVA – Selfless activity done for realization of BHAGAWAN i.e. The Eternal Supreme.
118   VATSA – Author's brother.
119   THIRUPPAVAI - Goddess Andal's poems.
120   PASURAM – Songs written in praise of Lord Vishnu, by 12 ALWARS, Greatest Devotees of Lord Vishnu, Goddess Andal is one of them.

they can share the same joy that we experience while learning more about the therapeutic experiences that benefitted WBH patients and their loved ones. We wish you the very best in your future endeavors and appreciate the time you were able to share with us. Please feel free to contact us if you are ever back in town on occasion and would like to visit. Thank you again, Christina, West Bloomfield Hospital, Michigan".

"Gayatri, I landed safely, did you eat?" asked my brother.

"It was very good, Vatsa. Did Bharat tell you that we have decided to go back to Sydney?", I asked.

From this time onwards, although my Thapas became vigorous, I also started to understand the real purpose of karma. Some learn by just hearing, and some by observing. I learnt through experience that I must not react but just be a witness for all experiences, be alert and vigilant so I don't create more karma.

The same food that we eat every day, suddenly for unknown reasons, can create problems on certain days. It's the same food, same ingredients, same method of cooking, however our body rejects it on some days. The body that followed our instructions yesterday, rejects it today. This is the nature of our physical body.

Sometimes, it has to fight against something, and other times it sends wrong signals to our system.

It has its limitations, it's of a changing nature and is subjected to modification. It can go wrong and will go wrong. And this is only due to my past karmas. As Swami Ramana Maharishi says, the other name for our "SHAREERAM" (body) is "VYADHI" (disease).

Like how a frog stuck in a well tries to climb two steps and slips five steps. When "I" the individual while trying to exhaust the "PrArabdha[121]" karma in this birth also ends up accumulating more and more every day, every minute.

How do I exhaust all my karmas? Through intense Bhakthi, I can get rid of all my "Sanchitha[122]" karmas. And like the frog, while experiencing the "Prarabdha" karma, I will keep acquiring more and more karmas.

How will I get rid of all these? Complete Surrender of Ego to The Supreme can only be the answer.

And the process of "Deeksha" i.e., initiation, allows the disciple to action this and blossom in their spiritual development. Guru, through the initiation, gives the disciple the "Adhikara" i.e., the right to chant the powerful mantras so that the disciple gets completely purified, and gets the single-pointed focus.

Bhakthi is critical in every phase of our journey and it must only grow stronger. Guru is the physical reality. All we have to do is Chant the Mantra with Bhakthi and the guru's instructions will make it work.

I got ready for the ritual called "Pancha Samskara[123]".

---

121   PRARABDHA KARMA - The Karmas that has started to yield its effects.
122   SANCHITA KARMA - All the Karmas that we have accumulated so far, i.e. in our past lives and this life.
123   PANCHA SAMSKARAM – "PANCHA" means 5 and "SAMSKARAM" means process of purifying. 5 activities that happen during this process are heated impressions on hands, wearing the symbol on 12 parts of the body, accepting the new name given to us by Acharya, learning the secret mantra & learning the process to worship "EMPERUMAN" i.e., Lord Vishnu and Goddess Mahalakshmi daily at home.

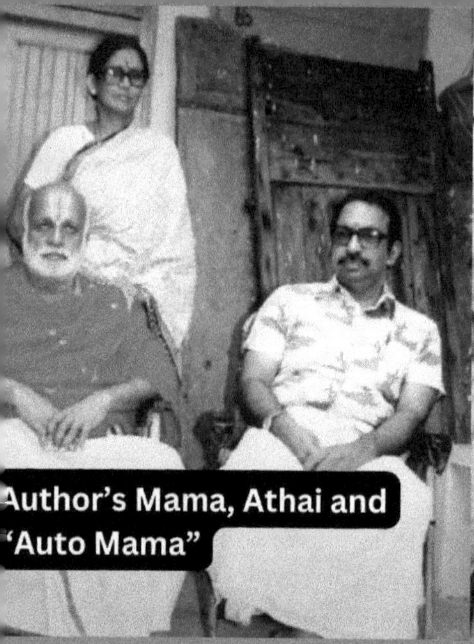

Author’s Mama, Athai and “Auto Mama”

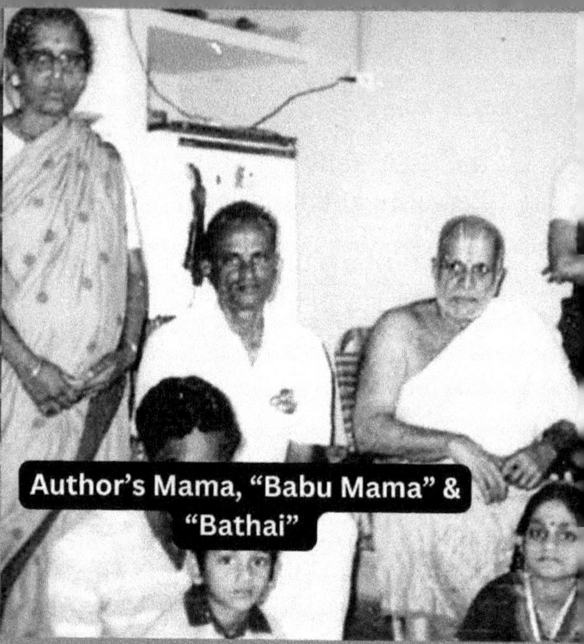

Author’s Mama, “Babu Mama” & “Bathai”

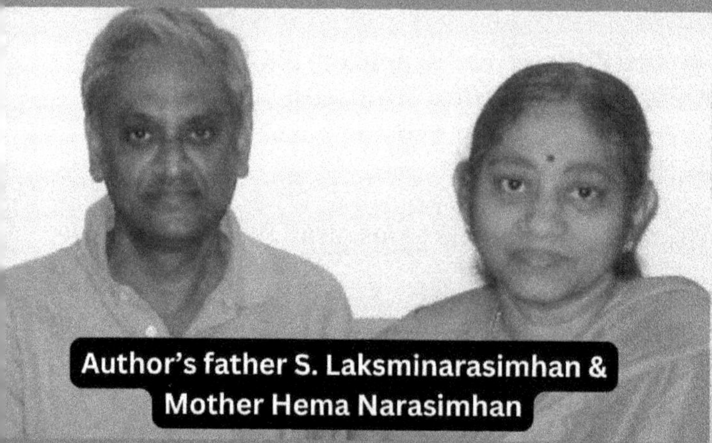

Author’s father S. Laksminarasimhan & Mother Hema Narasimhan

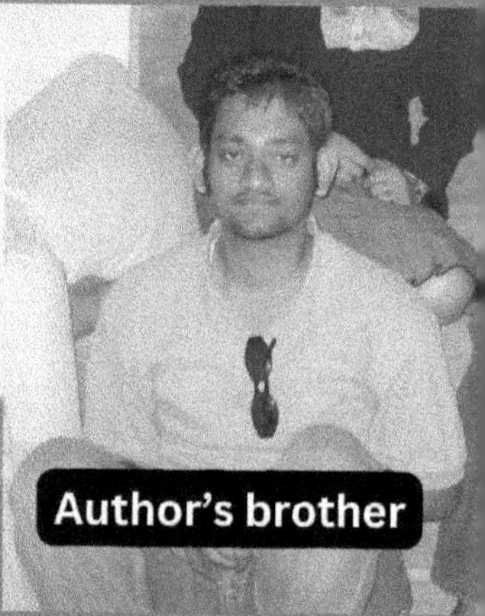

Author’s brother

Author’s Grandmother Ambujam & Grandfather COMPOSER KUMARAMANGALAM SRINIVASARAGHAVAN

Author with her husband

Author’s uncle Sridhar

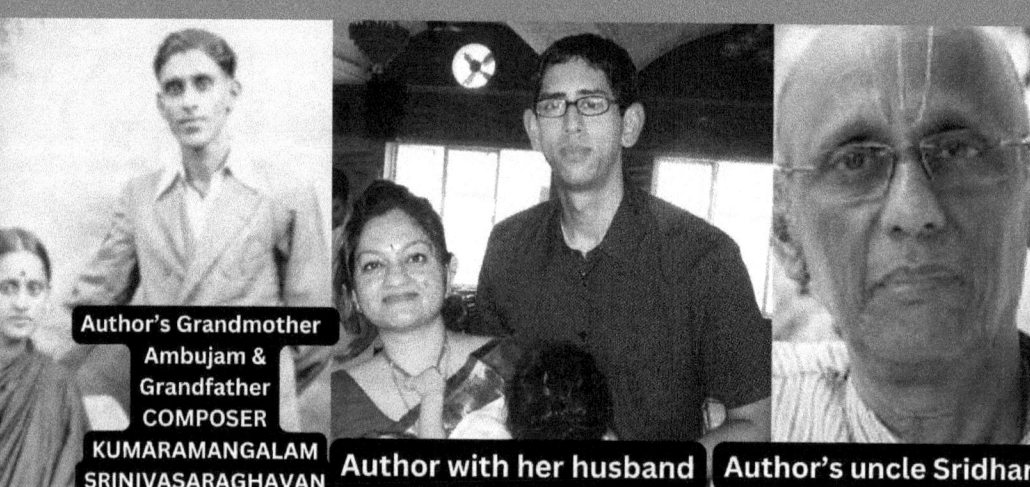

CHAPTER 5

SURRENDER

அகலகில்லேன் இறையுமென்று அலர்மேல்
மங்கை உறை மார்பா

நிகரில் புகழாய் உலகம் மூன்றுடையாய்
என்னை ஆள்வானே

நிகரில் அமரர் முனிக்கணங்கள்
விரும்பும் திருவேங்கடத்தானே

புகல் ஒன்றில்லா அடியேன் உன் அடிக்கீழ்
அமர்ந்து புகுந்தேனே

> Swami Nammazhawar says - "Oh Lord Srinivasa, Goddess Mahalakshmi, will NOT be away from You even for a fraction of a second and stays in Your Chest always !! You are an unparalleled and unbounded famous Lord! You have all three worlds to your possession! My Ruler! The peerless dEvAs and rishis worship You, pay obeisance to You, and desire You at TirumalA. I,- the one who has no other means and no one else for my redemption except you and only you- your eternal servant and only yours- hereby surrender at your lotus feet. you should bless me and take me to be at your lotus feet for ever.
> - **Swami NAMMAZHWAR**

ERADICATING THE KARMAS[124]

"Turn around, let me fix it" athai adjusted my madisar[125]. It was 3.30 in the morning. We left the car and we were patiently waiting at the Andavan Ashramam[126], looking forward to the Pancha Samskaram, a ritual that the Acharyan[127] does to the disciple and it involves five important Vedic techniques for the overall upliftment of the Atma. This is an initiation into the "Sri Vaishnava[128]" sampradaya.

While we were waiting, Acharya asked me to sing, I started the composition "Azhaga[129]" in the raga Sudha dhanyasi and when I went into the line "Nadandhu Nadandhu[130]" I decided to let go.

I entered into the Consciousness of myself, I was with the Acharyan however was not. Everything around me transformed into a dream world, I was overjoyed, Parashakthi's hands waiting to give me, she is indeed beautiful, she is Pure Consciousness and Supreme bliss, however as always, she disappeared.

What I really wanted was to experience that RASA again, that sweet RASA of transcendental love; however, she disappeared once again. I accepted reality.

I could see my Acharyan smiling at me. I cherish that smile every day, every minute. Was he trying to remind me of my Sanchita Karma?

---

124   KARMA – Actions, both good & bad.
125   MADISAR - A special saree worn on special occasions. This is generally followed in South India.
126   ANDAVAN ASHRAMAM – Acharya's place in Chennai, Tamil Nadu.
127   ACHARYAN – Guru, H.H. Srimadh Srirangaramanuja Mahadesikan Shree Mushnam Andavan. Refer https://www.andavan.org/our-previous-acharyas/srimad-srimushnam-andavan/ for more details.
128   SRI VAISHNAVA SAMPRADAYA –refers to a tradition where "Sri " i.e., Goddess Mahalakshmi and Lord Vishnu are worshiped as the Supreme.
129   AZHAGA – A composition of a Carnatic composer Ambujam Krishna, who lived in the 19th century.
130   NADANDHU – I walked to your temple, in Tamil.

Acharyan embossed the impressions of Shankam[131] & Chakram[132] on my left and right arms & gave me the "Deeksha".

I was very fortunate to receive the Rahasya Traya[133] mantras from him and this became another important turning point in my spiritual journey.

From this stage onwards, these Mantras also became my Prana[134].

With great dedication and devotion, I constantly did the "Japam[135]" for many years.

And this is when my "Thayar[136]" also came into my life to guide me.

She completely helped me in my inner transformation.

131	SHANKAM	– Conch of Lord Vishnu.
132	CHAKRAM	– Discus of Lord Vishnu.
133	RAHASYA THRAYAM	- Secret Mantras.
134	PRANA	– Cause of all energies.
135	JAPAM	– Chant.
136	THAYAR	- Goddess Mahalakshmi.

DREAMS

"Please sing the "Santhabara Pandariche[137]" Tonight for the Abhang concert," my mridangist requested.

I couldn't refuse. I knew I'd get those dreams again.

It's always the same dream for this particular Abhang, a dream of a very soothing, extremely beautiful dark blue complexion Mahakali, however, I felt incredibly peaceful, she was in her wild hair and youthful body, she looked stunning.

Again, I woke up with my body slightly shaking for a few moments. It was not scary, but rather an extremely peaceful feeling. This dream only happens when I sing this specific Abhang of Jani.

Why Kali? Why not Panduranga[138]? It's always been a mystery for me.

I will share with you, what I noticed in Jani's[139] Abhangs. For her, everything from food to bed is Vittala[140], she calls him "Vithabai" a feminine form of the masculine name "VITTALA"!

Is VITTALA the feminine form of the divine PARASHAKTHI, and that's indeed the eternal truth, as per "DASA MAHA VIDHYA[141]" Krishna is Kali and Kali is Krishna. And as per Jagath Guru Adi Sankaracharya's "SOUNDARYA LAHIRI" Mahakali is the "Gopala Sundari[142]"

Her Abhangs show me both Dvaita & Advaita, Saguna & Nirguna, Bhakthi & Gnyana, and fascinatingly Vaishnavam & ShAktham.[143]

137 SANTHBARA PANDARICHE - An Abhang of Sant Janabai.
138 PANDURANGA - Lord Vittala (A form of Lord Vishnu)
139 JANABAI - Women saint from Maharashtra.
140 VITTALA – A form of Lord Vishnu.
141 DASA MAHA VIDYA - 10 revered forms of Goddess.
142 GOPALA SUNDARI - Mahakali is Half Krishna and Half Lalithatripurasundari.
143 DWAITA, ADWAITA SAGUNA, NIRGUNA, BHAKTHI, GNYANAM, VAISHNAVAM, SHAKTHAM - Different philosophies, & the path to supreme.

She is angry with Vittala in some Abhangs, and in some, she feels sorry for him and becomes his mother. Her life was a beautiful blend of Bhakthi Yoga and Karma Yoga, she controlled her body, breath, mind, desires, her ego and finally reached the state of Mukthi through her Abhangs. Wish I could also.

Isn't she the embodiment of the goddess of wisdom, and a union of both the masculine and feminine aspects within a Yogini?

She taught me to step back, let go, just observe, and continue to experience Vittala without expecting anything in return.

"Sari evvare was nice," Bharat said when we got into the car. It was a composition in Ragam Sahana on Sita Ma. That very night, I had a strange dream featuring a King who looked like Shivaji Maharaj saluting a guru, and the guru suddenly transformed into a widow and uttered the words ``pavana rama.'' All I could recall from that dream was this phrase.

In the following months, I grappled with the recurring dream, desperate to understand its meaning. I resorted to chanting the Hanuman Chalisa[144], fervently requesting Hanuman's guidance in unraveling the mystery.

After many weeks of devoted chanting, I finally uncovered the truth: the mystic woman in my dreams was none other than a devout follower of Shivaji Maharaj's guru, Samartha Ramadas.

Although I had never heard of a Sant Veni Bai, it was she who had appeared in my dreams, and the Abhang belonged to her.

I was confident that if I set this to tune and sing and share, Parashakthi would be pleased, I did.

Was she? I don't know. I didn't get the experience that I was longing for.

144   HANUMAN CHALISA - A devotional song in praise of Lord Hanuman written by 15th century Sant Goswami Tulsidas in the Awadhi language.

Although I was able to quickly go into that space of transcendence through my music on various occasions, various concerts, various compositions, and various Ragas, it was the ecstasy of divine union that I was longing for.

And I knew that only Parashakthi could walk me through that space. She didn't. She had a reason.

She was helping me through my dreams.

At this stage of my spiritual journey, my intelligence was awakened by her grace, so I started understanding & interpreting my dreams.

Everything that happens in our life is for a reason, it is due to our karma. So, I surrendered and waited.

One Sunday evening, I had just come home from the studio after singing the lines from Abirami Andhadhi [145] "kan kalikkumpadi kandukonden.. Emperumattithan Perazhage" in the Ragam Dharmavathi.

We quickly had our dinner, and went to sleep.

"How can I describe your beauty, who are you?" I asked. "You called me "Perazhage[146]", here I am! Go find your Mithra."

"MITHRA[147]!"

How will I find my "Mithra"? I woke up, once again feeling lonely.

---

145   ABIRAMI ANDHADHI – A collection of poems in Tamil, sung on Goddess Abhirami, by a devotee Abhirami. Bhattar who lived in the 18th century.
146   PERAZHAGE – means "most beautiful" in Tamil.
147   MITHRA – Friend.

CHAPTER 6

CONCLUSION

> *All music is only the sound of His laughter,*
> *All beauty the smile of His passionate bliss;*
> *Our lives are His heart-beats, our rapture the bridal*
> *Of Radha and Krishna, our love is their kiss.*
> **- Sri Aurobindo in his poem "Who"**

MITHRA

Woke up, confused, lonely.

That was a comment notification sound from my phone.

"Madam, I'm going through a health problem, can I please request you to set the Narasimha[148] Shabar[149] to tune, record & share with me, I would like to listen to this in your voice every day. Thank you" a devotee on YouTube

Is Parashakthi indicating that Lord Narasimha is my Mitra?

That evening after I finished recording the Shabar, I thought that my "Mithra" was Narasimha, and I tried singing the composition "Narasimha Nannu Brovave[150]" I decided to go into that transcendental state for the line "Nee japamu Ni Smarana" and I did.

That was a great joy, Parashakthi's hands once again waiting to take me in and she is indeed beautiful. She is Pure Consciousness and Absolute bliss, however as always, she disappeared immediately.

The next day I shared the Shabar song with the devotee who had requested it. She listened to it for a week and all her problems vanished and her health also became normal. She requested that I share it with the public. I refused to.

Who am I to refuse? Narasimha didn't like my selfish intentions. Dreams of Narasimha for many nights. Finally, I had to turn that video on for the public.

Who is my "Mithra"? Will I ever find my Mithra?

---

148   NARSIMHA – An incarnation of Lord Vishnu.
149   SHABAR – Powerful Mantras that are generally in a local dialect of India, believed to be part of the Nath Sampradaya.
150   NARASIMHA NANNU BROVAVE – This is a composition of Saint Thyagaraja who lived in the 17th century.

It's been two months. Who is my "Mithra"? Who will help me find my "Mithra"?

It was a Navaratri[151] concert at a Vinayaka[152] Temple, and I had planned to sing Carnatic compositions.

After I went on stage, I took the courage to sing a particular bhajan that I generally avoid singing in public. However, this time, I didn't worry about anyone, all I wanted to know was, who my "Mithra" was, I can't wait anymore.

It's a bhajan that gives the essence of Guru Bhakthi.

It has always given me unimaginable brilliant experiences, and I sing this only when I'm desperately in need of going beyond that transcendental state. And this was the reason why I avoided singing this in public.

Started the lines of Sant Gorakshanath's bhajan "Javunji".

I went into that state, however this time I witnessed something different, something unimaginable; I witnessed myself; I also witnessed a beautiful young boy with extremely glowing white skin smiling with mischief in his glowing eyes running towards me taking my hands on and playing "thattamalai[153]" with me and I was overjoyed, a few rounds we played and then "oh no" he disappeared.

This time I was not sad, I was content, convinced that I had identified my Mithra.

"Are you okay, Mummy?" I could feel my daughter's touch from behind.

To tackle a problem intellectually is very easy, however, to tackle it existentially is difficult, I have to live through it, go

---

151   NAVARATRI – Hindu festival to worship the 9 forms of Goddesses DURGA viz. Shailaputri, Brahmacharini, Chandraghanta, Kushmanda, Skandamata, Katyayani, Kalaratri, Mahagauri, Siddhidatri.
152   VINAYAKA – Another name of Lord Ganesha.
153   THATTAMAALAI - A special game played using hands. This is generally played in South India & Maharashtra.

through it, and allow myself to be transformed through it – I must go through the experiences, and only then the change will happen in me and then the awakening.

Unless I do something, I change, I have a different perspective to look at, I move in an altogether different dimension beyond the intellect, I can achieve nothing. This is an important lesson that I learnt in my spiritual journey.

Through surrender the whole existence started pouring into me from everywhere, receiving unknown, unbelievable, unexpected, never even dreamed of. I accepted, went into the very roots, and wanted the deepest experiences because anything experienced can only be transcended.

I realized that my music is a great mystery of many multidimensional energies.

Every Ragini became a vehicle for me and every Ragini helped me to go beyond. For my transcendence I used my own music.

My way of expressing supreme bliss is to sing. I express it from my heart. Supreme bliss is only a byproduct. I can't grab it directly; I have to approach it indirectly.

Bliss is not a phenomenon; it is a divine thing that happens and then goes. however the experience stays with me forever.

I also realized that blissfulness is the very nature of my music, and sometimes, becoming unaware is also blissful.

When I'm singing, my music might flow outward, however, my intense, expanded awareness moves inside me, and I'm constantly aware of the innermost core of it. And that becomes ecstasy.

I finished the concert and came home. I was overjoyed that I had identified my Mithra.

The next morning, I turned my tanpura on to sing a particular composition of Muthuswami Dikshitar who had written in praise of my Mithra. I prayed to Ragini and elaborated on her for a while and then moved on to the composition and rendered it with devotion forty-one times.

I went to sleep.

"Chant this Moola Mantra for this many times," said my mama, in my dreams.

What I got from him was the Moola (Seed) mantra of my Mithra.

Bhakthi is important in our spiritual journey. I realized that rituals are also equally important.

If I want to achieve something that is extremely divine, I must also be ready to move into an altogether different dimension beyond my intellect.

The process or the rituals are to be strictly followed. If the instruction is to chant a particular mantra for this many times, I must strictly follow that. This is where our "Shradha[154]" is being tested.

I made two sets of "sankalpam[155]", and did the Thapas of the Moola mantra for one whole mandalam[156]. I strictly followed the "VidhAn[157]".

When we make promises, we must be ready to do even the things that we don't like to do, and that's when the mantra becomes even more effective. This is because, we are telling the deity that "un ishtam, en ishtam[158]".

---

154   SHRADHA - Dedication, determination.
155   SANKALPAM – Promise.
156   MANDALAM – forty-one days.
157   VIDHAN – Instructions that were given to me.
158   UN ISHTAM YEN ISHTAM – Means "Your wish is my wish" in Tamil.

I never wanted to share my spiritual journey with anyone BUT I had to make it one of my promises.

I received my Mithra. He became part of me, and then he grew within me, instigating a profound transformation that expanded my Consciousness. Then on that beautiful auspicious "Ashtami[159]"day, Mithra, alongside Parashakthi, stood ready to grant me my deepest desires.

He helped me experience that essence of separation, earliest affection, earliest love between me & my "ishta-deivam" which sprang from some previous cause.

He helped me smell the divine sweat, the divine fragrance of my ishta-deivam's "peethambaram[160]" that he was wearing on his waist, the only thing that I passionately desired for many years, the smell, the RASA of "purva-raga[161]", THROUGH THE LINES OF GODDESS ANDAL who had possessed me, "பெருமான் அறையில் பீதக வண்ண ஆடை கொண்டு[162]".

And at that moment, that divine sweat, that divine fragrance was an ecstasy of happiness, the ecstasy of separation, ecstasy exhibited before my meeting, a state of divine love anxieties, a state of the unimaginable union, however, this time I was not afraid of being separated from his beautiful smiling eyes.

Thank you, Mithra.

---

159   ASHTAMI – An auspicious day.
160   PEETHAMBARAM – Gold/yellow colored cloth. Lord Krishna's favorite.
161   PURVA RAGA - One of the states of VIPRALAMBHA i.e., separation.
162   பெருமான் அறையில் பீதக வண்ண ஆடை கொண்டு - Goddess ANDAL PASURAM.

GANESHA

GORAKSHANATH

MURUGA

THYAGARAJA

SARASWATHI

RAMA

KALLAZHAGAR

PURANDARA DASA

MEERABAI

AKKA MAHADEVI

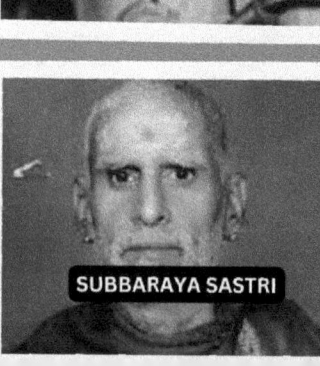
SUBBARAYA SASTRI

H. H.H SRIRANGARAMUJA
SRIMUSHNAM ANDAVAN

REQUEST TO THE READER

Dear cherished reader, Thank you so much for being a significant part of my life and joining me on my spiritual journey.

If you've found value in your reading or listening experience today, I humbly ask that you take a brief moment right now to leave an honest review of this book. It won't cost you anything but 30 seconds of your time—just a few seconds to share your thoughts with others.

Your voice can go a long way in helping someone else find the same inspiration and knowledge that you have.

Are you familiar with leaving a review for an Audible, Kindle, or e-reader book? If so, it's simple:

If you're on Audible: just hit the three dots in the top right of your device, click rate & review, then leave a few sentences about the book along with your star rating.

If you're reading on Kindle or an e-reader, simply scroll to the last page of the book and swipe up—the review should prompt from there.

If you're on a Paperback or any other physical format of this book, you can find the book page on Amazon (or wherever you bought this) and leave your review right there.

Thank you.

Milton Keynes UK
Ingram Content Group UK Ltd.
UKHW050945270324
440141UK00009B/100